SOME COMMENTS
FROM OUR BRILLIANT CLIENTS

"Client feedback from our proposals has been incredible. The tracking enables us follow up at the right time, helping us win more business"

Simon Banks - Tallboy Communications

"Our business is built around this product. Everything we do from keeping in touch, to sending quotes and raising invoices is done through Business Automation CRM"

Joakim Roth - Light Foot LED

"Our Business Automation System has revolutionised the way we think of our leads, prospects and clients now. It's so easy to see exactly what's going on with any contact at a second's notice."

Matt Hunt - OLOVES

"Justin brilliantly analysed Nu Beginnings' CRM requirements, provided a fantastic solution. We've saved hours each week in admin and a large sum of money in annual fees. Great service and excellent attention to detail"

Samantha-Leigh Harper - Nu Beginnings

"Feedback from the staff has been incredible. Having everyone working from the same system is so much more efficient. Clients love the way we send documentation now through the proposal system. It really makes us stand out."

Claire Tyne - MAA Architects

"Business Automation CRM allows us more time to focus on the core activities of our business. The ongoing support and service has been exemplary. If you are a company looking to improve your workflow, processes and efficiency I would sign up"

Robert Baggs - Berkshire Wealth

"Business Automation CRM allows me and my staff to keep in touch with prospects and clients that would otherwise have slipped into thin air. The value of simply following up effectively has paid for the system already."

Tom Aitken - Enhance Services

"I find preparing quotes really easy to do. When sending quotes it appears far more credible which improves our perception as a business"

James Coakes - Organise Events

"Since using the system, it's integrated with our processes seamlessly. It helps us minimise the menial tasks and completely automate everything which means I've got more time to do the things important to me"

Jack Manley - Freestyle Web Design

"Communicating effectively with my readers, prospects and clients is the most important part of my business. Keeping all this information up-to-date in separate systems is a nightmare. In my Business Automation System, it's all in one place and I can email, from a beautifully branded template, to any segment of my database."

Tim Coe - myUSP

"My proposals look beautiful and blow my competition out the water. I win so many more jobs than I used to. Amazing!"

Amanda Lucas - Amanda Lucas Photography

"Business Automation CRM literally saved my life. It handles all my customers, who's been to what parties, when and where. I can handle my more official documents through the proposal system and have my contracts signed in minutes instead of weeks"

Garth Hill - Pinpoint Music Group

"Being able to run my entire business from my phone has given me a new perspective on how I run it. I now have the visibility to see my business statistics and how much my staff are achieving."

Ben Stringer - Sussex Academy of Music

"Using the Online Proposal System we've won far more business than we would have otherwise. Being able to see when, what and how long someone's read our proposals for is vital. I can now follow up at the perfect time and win the business. Genius!"

Bradley Jones - Printergage

AUTOMATE YOUR BUSINESS

AUTOMATE YOUR BUSINESS

THE BUSINESS OWNER'S GUIDE TO
A SIMPLER BUSINESS THAT RUNS ITSELF

ADAM HEMPENSTALL

SPECIAL THANKS TO...

Tim Coe who convinced me to focus on Business Automation,

Ben and Rob at Sussex Academy of Music who took a leap of faith and let us build the first Business Automation System,

Sabrina for being such a consistently brilliant business partner and taking care of clients while I work on projects like this,

and to every client who's ever paid me a penny…

I love you all.

TABLE OF CONTENTS

1:	Your business problems	15
2:	Design your business from scratch	24
3:	Why you should use web based software	33
4:	Introducing some web based systems we use	40
5:	Automate your marketing	52
6:	Automate your sales	71
7:	Automate your workflow	92
8:	Automate your finances	106
9:	Automate yourself	114
10:	Evolution	129

IS THIS BOOK FOR YOU?

This book is for the small business owner who feels like their business runs them, not the other way round. It's for the business owner who's starting early, finishing late at night and spends their entire time thinking about work and feels they have a job not a business.

It's for business owners who need some way to organise their business but don't know where to turn, what systems to use or how to set them up.

It's for entrepreneurs who are building businesses and need to set them up the right way so they're not required to be there, are scalable and can grow faster.

It's for the IT guy who wants to steal all my good ideas and sell them to his clients for an obnoxious markup. ;-)

Lastly, it's for our clients who I personally see struggle, working far too hard on admin and not spending nearly enough time on revenue generating tasks.

This book will make you a business owner again.

Adam Hempenstall

Founder of Advantix

Introduction

MY STORY
AND WHY YOU NEED THIS BOOK

Think back to the last time you called a massive corporation. It's actually pretty amazing what happens when you give them your account number and in an instant, they can tell you everything about your account. We take it for granted how amazing that really is! This always fascinated me but as I started building my web design company, Advantix, back in the mid 2000's I realised how many smaller companies didn't have this kind of incredible technology, and couldn't help but think they needed it.

For as long as I can remember, I've always wanted to build my own house. Now more than ever I can see that becoming a reality. One thing's for sure, if you're going to build a house with your friends, in a place where there's no Internet connection because it's a building site, it might be tricky to run a client based Internet business. It was important to me that when I built Advantix, it could run without me if it needed to.

Over the years I was fortunate enough to build up a pretty successful website design company, not by adding staff members, but rather by putting systems in place to automate tasks so we could focus on generating revenue. Some of our web clients wanted to use some of the tools we'd built, so as one thing led to another we started building these tools and systems for them too.

Then the conversation that changed everything...

A business mentor and friend of mine, Tim Coe, and I were chatting on the phone at about 2am one morning back in 2010 about the progress we'd both made in business. I remember it like it was yesterday... He went off on some massive diatribe about how we're not a web design company, we're a business automation company, and how all of the effort we were putting in to get people marginal differences with their websites could be focused on the idea of turning around entire businesses with the systems we can build. He'd been saying it for years, the rest of our clients had been telling me for years by asking for it. It was time to change so we simply stopped doing web design and solely focused all our efforts on Business Automation.

As it turns out, there's not a single company that we've found that are doing the same kind of work we are. I feel like it's my personal obligation to completely dominate this category of work. No-one else is stepping up, so it might as well be us. We renamed our company from Advantix to The Business Automation Company, and we were off. Since that time we've taken what we've learned, put it on steroids, strapped a rocket launcher to it and blasted it into the stratosphere! Anyone we work with finds themselves depending on our systems the same way people depend on mobile phones. I've heard it so many times: "I have no idea how I'd manage without my system now"

By the end of this book, my hope is that you will feel the same way.

What you will learn in this book

Like with all major changes to any business, there is a process to it. My hope is you can start seeing a pretty dramatic shift in your personal and business productivity within a number of days if you go through the exercises.

The first thing we'll do is take a look at the problems your business is facing, so we know the areas to focus on. Next we'll lay the foundations for the kinds of systems you'll need.

We'll then take a look at the types of software that will work for your business, so you can start setting them up.

Then in turn, we'll look at a whole avalanche of ways you can automate your Marketing, Sales, Workflow, Finances and finally Yourself.

I've deliberately kept this book simple to understand and easy to action. I honestly believe you can revolutionise your business in a weekend dedicated to this. It sounds like a real commitment, and it is, but it's really a very small price to pay for changing your business life.

Chapter 1

Your Business Problems

"A problem well stated is a problem half solved"
Chris Howard - Founder of Academy of Wealth and Achievement

A NEW WAY OF THINKING
ABOUT STARTUP BUSINESSES

Back in the old days a "start-up" was a business planning to launch. They would sort their market research, marketing, customer database, shop front, suppliers - everything. THEN they would launch the business. Today we take the toddler approach if we're starting a service business, which seems to be "learn the ropes as you go".

The danger of doing this is that we rarely set everything up before we launch. Maybe you get a website and some business cards, or a brochure, and then cruise along for a year or two. Here is the problem though - there is no 'set point' at which you're supposed to get your business systems in place and get it all organised. It all happens too gradually - it's kind of like becoming overweight. You don't suddenly wake up and figure out you're 23 stone; it's a gradual process that you don't notice day-to-day unless someone points it out to you. Even then you might remain in denial.

With any gradual issue, there's always a tipping point. Maybe you can't suddenly get into that pair of jeans; or in this case you might miss an appointment, forget to call someone back or miss out on a massive deal. I'd like you to challenge yourself, and make the decision to do something about this before you run yourself into the ground. There's no need to wait.

In this book there are exercises and instructions which, when you've finished, will give you a set of systems to help you stay focused on revenue generating tasks and not stressing about those essential but menial admin tasks.

It's so unbelievably easy to set these things up, you have absolutely no excuse at all. A really good solid evening working on this will get you most the way there; or ideally a weekend away from the office on a laptop to set it all up.

The result will be as if you've had an IT professional come into your business and install millions of pounds worth of software. I don't use those massive figures to impress you, I use them to represent the value of some of the free technology I'm going to introduce you to later in this book. After all that, you'll be working less hours and growing your business faster. Before we do anything though, we need to identify some problems.

Let's have a look at some of the common problems you might be facing as a small business owner, who has no systems in place to keep things in order:

- Missing appointments
- Post-it notes everywhere
- Don't have any of your customers' details in a single place
- Your reminder system consists of scrap pieces of paper
- Communication breakdown within the business
- You're spending all your mornings, evenings and weekends working on admin
- Invoicing and writing proposals is a dreaded task
- You're stressed beyond belief and know the business can't grow in the state it's in.

Let me be direct with you. It's up to YOU to sort this out. In this book are tons of ideas, tricks, software recommendations (free or super cheap), which will help you regain control, increase production and grow revenue without adding more staff. Unfortunately, no-one is going to come along and do this for you. Want another wake-up call? If you think this is bad, at what point is it suddenly going to get better?

- When you have more money? - Nope! Just more pressure and more work.
- When you employ someone? - No way! You have to train them and go through all sorts of red tape and nonsense just to have them there.
- It'll fix itself in time? - Really? Has it fixed itself yet? Nope.
- When you go on holiday, you'll look at it then? - No you won't, you'll justify that you've worked hard and just sunbathe.

Face it... No external force is going to fix this for you. **This is 100% completely your job.** After all - this is what business owners are supposed to do! If it was easy, everyone would do it.

What Are Your Problems?

Whenever I offer any business advice in this area, it follows a very simple pattern: Discover all the problems you have (some you'll know about, some you won't), propose solutions and then put them into action. The problems are an essential starting point and cannot be ignored.

Our first ever Business Automation system came about almost by accident when I went into Sussex Academy of Music who were existing website clients at the time, and started having a conversation about their online shop at about 2pm. I can't really tell you how it happened but we spent the next 24 hours with all of us making notes and thinking of ways to improve their business. I had no idea that this would become my first ever Discovery Process. When we eventually took a break, we had over 30 pages of notes.

This served as the foundation for the system we would eventually build and work on for over 4 years.

This is one of the most important exercises you can do and I recommend you do this every 6 months or so. All we're going to do is just start identifying problems within your business - that's it. Not necessarily to the extent of what we did with Sussex Academy of Music but if that's what it takes - do it!

There aren't any limits or guidelines so anything like 'low sales' to 'Amy doesn't file the invoices properly' is the kind of thing we're looking for. What's important is that you think about all areas of your business and write down the problems for each. Some areas to think about:

- Time Management
- Order processing
- Customer service
- Internal processes
- Storing information
- File management
- Finance
- Reminders about important tasks
- Delegation
- Communication
- Work / Life Balance

These are by no means conclusive, just a few ideas to get you started. On the next two pages, just write as many problems as you can think of that you're currently facing in your business day-to-day. For the purpose of this exercise, a problem doesn't need to be a catastrophic disaster, but anything that you'd consider to be less than ideal.

Go for it... Do it now, don't skip over it or this entire book will be glorified bed-time reading and definitely not the revolutionary, life changing event I'm promising it will be.

YOUR BUSINESS PROBLEMS

YOUR BUSINESS PROBLEMS

That's great! Well done! This is going to serve as your guide for the rest of the exercises in this book and your quest for a simpler business.

SUMMARY
OF CHAPTER 1

In order to go forward, we need to take a look at the problems and use them as signposts. As business owners we're always going to experience issues in some form or another, but if we can try to make sure they're not time sucking problems that stop you earning money, then we stand a fighting chance of living the good life.

If you're busy and problems exist in your business, then you need something to sort them out. It's not magically going to sort itself out and the only person that can do it is you.

What we're going to be looking at next is how to start laying the foundations for an organised business.

Chapter 2

Design Your Business From Scratch

"Design is a funny word. Some people think design means how it looks. But of course, if you dig deeper, it's really how it works"

Steve Jobs - Co-Founder of Apple

YOU WILL NEED **SOMETHING** TO ORGANISE YOUR BUSINESS

Let's be clear about one thing. You need SOMETHING to organise your business. For the first year, if you have a client based service business, you can probably do this in your head; but when you get to about 30 clients you need something to keep track of the proposals you need to send, phone calls you need to make and tasks you need to complete. Unfortunately, most people I meet have 150-200 clients and STILL try to do this in their head; and they wonder why they forget stuff and their service ends up questionable.

Seriously, if you can't remember when you promised a client you'd complete their job for them, how can you expect to remember the information needed to make your customer interaction epic. Information like whether they play golf or not, how they take their tea and coffee, and other little things? Think about it - how much would it impress you if you walked into one of your supplier's offices and they welcomed you with "Latte with 2 sugars yes?" You'd be thinking, "how the hell do they know that?!" You would never go out of your way to remember information like that, but to look it up on a CRM 3 minutes before you walk in the door isn't overly difficult. What's the end result? You feel like their best customer ever. That is without doubt, the easiest "extra mile" customer service in history. You can do the same thing and it's as simple as making a note in a system which takes about 15 seconds in real time which you can do from your phone.

Let's get computers to do the work shall we?

It's important that you start considering the possibility that unless you physically need to touch something, talk to someone over the phone or meet someone face to face, a computer could do some of your work for you. I know it can be hard to imagine, after all, how is a computer supposed to invoice someone for the correct amount, or send emails at the right time, or say the right thing? I'm here to tell you that it is all possible and actually very easy.

What we need to do is work out the flow of communication and information in your business.

To demonstrate, I'll explain the process at The Business Automation Company in the context of working with private clients, building custom Business Automation Systems. This entire process starts from the initial call and goes right the way through to the final invoice. This is to give you an idea of how a personal 1-1 service business can be automated. After, you'll be able make the same plan for your business.

Step 1: Marketing

First thing we do is have a website set up to attract people to sign up to receive this book. This starts a series of automated emails and offers them a chance to get some tailored advice. Their details go straight into our own Business Automation System.

My involvement: Signing a card and putting it in the post box (5 minutes)

Step 2: Sales

I'll meet the potential client, ask a pre-written set of questions to determine what they need, then put that into a proposal of which certain bits are also pre-written.

My involvement: 1 meeting (2 or 3 hours)

Step 3: Invoicing

We very often suggest payment plans over a number of months, all for varying amounts, so we use Xero to automatically send the invoices on the correct dates. The initial process takes about 5 minutes and I don't need to worry about billing them again.

My involvement: 2 minutes

Step 4: Monthly Payments

We use GoCardless to manage all of our direct debits. We take the relevant details from the customer and set it up once, then there's never an issue again.

My involvement: 2 minutes

Step 5: Production

Our project manager, Sabrina, and I will have a meeting where we will plan out the project. We set the project up in Basecamp where I can check in at any time on how that project is doing should a client want an update.

My involvement: A few hours

Step 6: Support

We use email for support but the majority of requests, go directly to the team that deal with the enquiry. We then respond to keep quality control high.

My involvement: Zero

You see how many things happen, yet I'm totally detached from them unless I want to be involved. Consider that the systems I'm talking about here range from £5,000 - £25,000. My involvement, while valuable and vital is remarkably low. Having so much of this being pre-produced, automated and delegated allows me to focus my time where it's needed, instead of having a scattered approach and trying to do everything myself.

Remember - at any point, I can interrupt the system and get involved if I choose to. It's not "set it, forget it, AND NEVER SEE IT AGAIN". You can always go back and edit these things if they're not quite right, but the point is to set them up and focus on other things. An often forgotten point here is how much better an automated system is for your customers.

Consider our support system. It's actually a massive selling point now. Before, clients would send in requests in all sorts of different ways causing a customer service nightmare. It took what was potentially a straight forward situation because someone found an error or someone wants a quote on a new feature, and made it into a long drawn out process.

Compare that to now where they fill in a few answers from right within their system, and the relevant person deals with it the second it happens. This has taken us completely out of the system and removed us as a bottleneck. This is something we show people in presentations now as, while it's nothing revolutionary, it shows we have systems in place to keep things simple and efficient. In addition, as our client list grows, we can put more people on the development and bug fixing end of the support system without changing anything else.

Data you never had before

Once you start using systems to do tasks, it's amazing how much more information you have access to. Using our support system as an example again, we can now see all sorts of new information like the average fix time, how long people take to approve quotes, and which people report which kinds of errors (often indicating they need more training in a certain area). This kind of information gives you power to make informed decisions based on facts, instead of guessing.

EXERCISE:
PRODUCING YOUR WORKFLOW

Okay, so we've taken a look at some of the ways we automate the flow of someone buying something, now you do the same. Here's how I recommend you do it.

1. Simply list all the "exchanges" that take place. This could be people receiving your marketing, meetings, phone calls, emails, ordering, approval - anything (you don't need the explanation I gave for each one).

2. Put them in the order that they happen (look at ours as a guide).

3. Think about your level of involvement at each stage and remember that, unless it requires you to physically be there interacting with someone, or making something, then it can probably be automated.

Write this up on the next page. This will serve as a roadmap for later on, but it's important you do this now or the next bit of the book won't make much sense. It will probably take you 90 seconds. Go.

YOUR WORKFLOW

SUMMARY
OF CHAPTER 2

In this chapter we've looked at trying to lay some ground work so you can plan out which parts of your business need attention.

Once you've done the exercise in this chapter, you'll identify all the different elements of your business and you'll start to see where you can be removed.

In the next chapter, I'm going to give you an introduction to the types of software you can use to start automating the sections of your business you just identified.

Chapter 3

Why You Should Use Web Based Software

"How could I handle work on a day like today?"
Ferris Bueller - Legend

THE HOLIDAY FROM HELL
OR WAS IT?

A little story... I was in Tenerife enjoying a nice 4 week break from the day-to-day of business (while it kept running as if I was there), and the phone rang while at dinner. It was the Police. They told me my apartment had been broken into and looked like the place had been robbed. I couldn't help but feel relieved that my family hadn't been butchered or something. I lost two TVs, two games consoles, and two of our computers.

While the TVs and games consoles being stolen were annoying, they were certainly replaceable. For most other businesses, the loss of the computers would have been catastrophic. In our case, it didn't make a single bit of difference.

Why?

Everything was stored online! Our accounts, our customer database, our contracts, our customer's system files. All we needed to do was replace the computers when we got home, log back into those sites and we were back up and running again.

If I had everything stored at home physically on those computers, the whole business would have been screwed. I would have lost everything... including my mind.

Why am I telling you this?

The reason it didn't matter is because all our systems are web-based. So what does it mean if something is web-based (sometimes known as 'web apps')? It simply means that it is software designed using web technology. In basic terms, it's a big complicated website. The benefits of this are endless! What I want you to try to do by the end of this book is have as many of your business systems as possible being web-based. You don't have to use the systems we recommend, they're just what we use. Feel free to search for your own.

Need some convincing to use web-based systems as opposed to desktop software, which you install on single computers?

Cheaper: Traditional software is more expensive to build, test, maintain, upgrade and install. Since competition in web technology is huge, it pushes the price down massively and there's nothing to install, also saving distribution costs.

Faster to upgrade: Because of the lengthy testing procedures involved in traditional software you'd install, this delays the upgrading. Traditional software often has annual or bi-annual updates. However, since developers can test web-based software on the fly, the second it's working, it's live; so updates take minutes or hours, not months and years

Stored Offsite: The databases behind the software are backed up by an external hosting company, very often multiple times a day and are stored offsite. If there was a fire and your computer burned down, it crashed or someone stole it, you wouldn't lose any of the data stored online. It's by far the safest method of backups.

No Installing: There's nothing to install. Because it essentially acts like a website, all you need is a computer and an Internet connection to log in. Everything else is already set up for you, and is the same wherever you are.

No IT Person: Unless you have a massive office and team, and need a full-time IT person anyway, you don't really need one. This alone will save you at least £30,000 a year or £250 a month for a contract IT company.

Integrations: Integrating traditional software is as good as impossible these days. With web-based software, it can sometimes be just a click of a button. There's a huge business around just integrating software together. Take advantage of this.

Incentives: Running a successful web-based software business is among one of the most ideal business models ever. Regular monthly income in exchange for providing a service which costs next to nothing to maintain after it's built and working. This means all the development team and business owner have to do all day is build new features on the back of suggestions from paying customers. The service usually only ever gets better and you pay a small monthly cost which is likely to stay the same.

"I couldn't run my business without web-based software"

I couldn't run my business without web-based software and going forward 2, 3, 5, or even 10 years, it's going to get harder and harder to manage without it. I spend roughly 2-3 months of my year abroad yet no-one ever notices. I can get away with this because there is a set of systems under me which manages 90% of the business. I can check on everything from wherever I want by just logging into our different web-based systems. Even if there isn't desktop Internet, most of the services we use have iPhone apps anyway. The more I travel, the more I'm finding that there really aren't very many occasions where you can't find Internet access.

If it isn't obvious by now that I think web-based software should be the heart of your business, then I should give up writing. I want to explain the different types of systems which you could choose to help you organise your business. I've distilled it down to 3 major types.

1. Microsoft Excel (Desktop Software):

This point includes other desktop software like Microsoft Word. This will store information in a disorganised way and not remind you of anything. It's basically the same as writing it down on a piece of paper and filing it *neatly* under the sofa.

2. Off The Shelf Web-Based Systems:

Considerably better as they can be set up instantly and can automate certain parts of your business. The only downside is you may need to adapt your business slightly to suit the software. The cost of off-the-shelf systems are often so low, it's quite possible to run even a decent sized business for a few hundred pounds a month.

3. Custom Business Automation System:

This will automate huge chunks of your processes to the point where you will save on average 15-20 hours a week personally of admin work and allow you to focus on growth and revenue. It will also act as a centralised hub as all the components of your company are built into the same system.

The idea being that in this day and age with modern technology, you shouldn't be spending your time manually creating invoices in Microsoft Word, or typing notes into Microsoft Excel or really using Microsoft anything! Word is great for writing letters and Excel is awesome for drawing pretty graphs, but both of these pieces of software are outdated and it's simply habit that keeps us using them, not necessity.

It's important to use the right tools for the job. The best way to do that is to take a look at your list of problems we wrote down in Chapter 1, then try and find software to fix those problems.

Now, the ideal is that you have something custom built. That would be where a team of professionals would figure out all your "business problems" then build something from scratch that solved every one of them. This is the more expensive option for sure, but not anywhere near what you'd expect.

I can't put every single business eventuality in this book so if you're reading this and thinking to yourself, "Okay, some great points but it's not entirely applicable to my business" then I'd like to be able to point you in the right direction. Just drop me an email to adam@businessautomation.co.uk, give me some details on your situation and I'll do my best to help you either by email, or over the phone.

SUMMARY
OF CHAPTER 3

Ending this chapter, the most important thing is realising that web-based software is the way to future proof your business and keep everything organised. On that subject, let me introduce you some systems you could use.

Chapter 4

Introducing Some Web Based Systems We Use

Disclaimer:

The prices of these systems are correct at the time of writing. Some of these are owned and managed by us, others aren't. What I would not do is recommend any product I don't use myself personally or in my business.

MAILCHIMP.COM

MailChimp

MailChimp is the answer to a small business' email marketing nightmare. It will manage all your email marketing efforts, from one off campaigns to autoresponders, segmenting your list and everything in between. It's designed for small businesses who want to be able to send bulk email campaigns but don't want it to take too much time, effort or money.

There are plenty of other email marketing software systems but I haven't found anything else that strikes the perfect balance of:

- Easy to use
- Cheap
- Full of great features

Cost: Free until you have 2000 subscribers

BUSINESSAUTOMATION.CO.UK/FREE

Business Automation CRM (Free)

If you currently use Microsoft Excel, ACT! or scraps of paper to organise your customer database, then at least get yourself signed up to the free Business Automation CRM.

It's a very trimmed down version of Business Automation CRM but it is free. You can store up to 100 contacts and send them proposals. There's no follow-up system, workflow management or marketing suite.

Cost: Free forever for 50 contacts

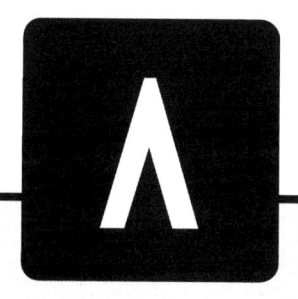

BUSINESSAUTOMATION.CO.UK

Business Automation CRM (Paid)

If you are running a service business, Business Automation CRM and the intricate setup service that comes with it will be perfect for you. Key features include:

- Your website enquiries automatically going into your CRM
- Being able to add notes, assign tasks and see a detailed buying history
- Send high converting proposals (Better Proposals built in)
- Follow up with everyone you need to without having to remember or think what to write and without it taking ages.
- Track your sales process from enquiry to sale.
- Automatically notify your client about milestones reached during workflow
- Create laser focused email marketing campaigns by using the data in the CRM to its fullest extent.

Cost: Depends on your situation.

BETTERPROPOSALS.CO.UK

Better Proposals

Sending better proposals is probably the easiest thing you can do to increase revenue. After all, it's the biggest factor in someone's decision in whether to choose you or a competitor.

Better Proposals gives you a way to send beautiful and professionally designed proposals in minutes. Beyond simply sending better looking proposals, your clients will now be able to digitally sign them which speeds up your sales process to no end.

Have you ever sent a proposal to a client and thought "Did they even get it? I'm not sure whether to follow up yet". Better Proposals tells you exactly when someone's opened, what they've read and how long for. This means you can follow up at a time that makes sense to you, not relying on guesswork.

Cost: Plans range from Free to £35 per month

SKYPE.COM

Skype

Skype has been around for what seems like forever at this point, and since Microsoft bought it, it's done little to no innovating. That said, it's still a brilliant tool when you're travelling.

For instance, I have an 0208 Skype-In number which rings my mobile and uses my data. Since (in Europe at least) this is more or less free, I can pick up calls from people thinking I'm in my "London office", when in reality I'm half way up a mountain in Croatia or sitting on a lake in Madrid.

If you travel a lot, get yourself a Skype Number. They're fantastic.

Cost: £3 a month

DOCS.GOOGLE.COM

Google Docs

You could consider Google Docs like Microsoft Office online, but better. The main differences being:

- You don't have to download any software.
- You can share your documents or spreadsheets with anyone free.
- You can both edit the document at the same time.
- Export as traditional files if you need to.

Cost: Free

DROPBOX.COM

Dropbox

Dropbox backs up your files and syncs them with all your devices. Let's say that you have a work computer and a home computer. You create a document on your home computer and save it in Dropbox (the same way you'd use 'My Documents'). Let's say you then go to work in the morning and want to access that file, you simply open Dropbox and you'll find it in the exact same state.

If you don't have Internet access, don't worry – it will sync all the files whenever it finds an Internet connection but since it downloads them constantly, it's just like opening a file in My Documents. When you connect back to the Internet again, it will re-sync the files you changed. It's so much safer from a file safety point of view, as it keeps old versions of files and it's backed up in multiple places.

Cost: 2gb storage is free

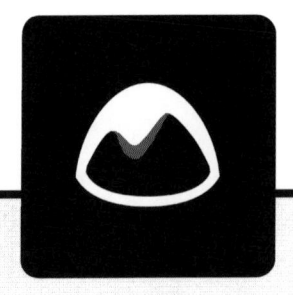

BASECAMP.COM

Basecamp

If your business sells a service that has a lot of intricate parts, then Basecamp might be worth looking at. It's a simple tool for keeping all of your projects and the related notes and files in one place. It allows you to:

- Create to-do lists
- Start discussions
- Add notes
- Assign tasks
- Collaborate with your team

We use Basecamp every day to manage the development of our clients' Business Automation Systems. For what we do, it would be very difficult to manage without a tool like this.

Cost: £12 upwards, depending on number of projects.

XERO.COM

XERO

Xero is online accounting software that really has taken the small business world by storm. Here are some of the more basic features:

- Keeping track of all your income and expenses
- See which of your invoices are overdue
- Add expenses on the go using their mobile app
- Repeat billing
- Invoice from wherever you are using their app
- Reconcile your statements in seconds

It automatically logs into your internet banking, grabs all your transactions and automatically recognises the ones you've entered before. The more it learns about your transactions, the less time it takes. If you do nothing else, give Xero a spin.

Cost: £12 - £24 a month

GOCARDLESS.COM

GoCardless

If you accept regular payments from your clients in any way then you owe it to yourself to explore what GoCardless has to offer. They have made collecting Direct Debits so unbelievably simple and easy.

You send your client a little link to fill in, where they create an account and put their account details in. This then gives you permission to take money from them.

Beyond monthly payments, you can take ad-hoc payments too. With this in mind, you don't actually need a monthly subscription business, you just need to do repeat business with them.

Cost: Free to set up, No monthly charges 1% transaction fee up to a maximum of £2.

SUMMARY
OF CHAPTER 4

These systems are what we use. It doesn't necessarily mean they are right for your business, although I'd argue that any business could at least use some of them. Do your own research and find systems that suit you, or contact me and I'll see if I know of anything more relevant to your specific situation.

Web-based software has primarily been used in the marketing world because it's almost impossible to do it manually. Most business owners don't seem to think about using the (mostly) free technology to do the same with other areas of their businesses.

Over the next 5 Chapters, that's exactly what I'm going to walk you through. Let's start at the beginning of any business transaction: Marketing.

Chapter 5

Automate Your Marketing

"Marketing is using the right technology to get the right message to the right person at the right time"

Frank Kern - Internet Marketer

WHY EMAIL MARKETING?

I recommend using Email Marketing because of its inherently automatable nature. You can achieve a similar thing with Direct Mail but it's not quite as "set it and forget it" as email, and it's certainly not as cheap.

Your Marketing Calendar

The last few years, we've done this to great effect. We sat down and thought about all of the products we were going to be launching, the content we wanted to get out there, the events we wanted to put on, and wrote a list of every email we wanted to send and put them in a list like this:

January:
- *3rd: Happy New Year*
- *12th: Blog post summary email*
- *25th: Free PDF on Business Automation*

Then, the same thing for February through to December. What I did next was go through and write all of these emails in one go, then design them. This might sound like a ridiculous task; when I mention this to people I'm often looked at like I just suggested head butting glass. The 2 objections are these:

Objection 1: "What the hell do I write about?"

If you're a service business, and you teach people anything at all, just think about all of the things you've taught in the last few months with private clients, and make a massive list. Split it into smaller sections if you have to - email content doesn't need to be that long.

Objection 2: "When am I going to find the time?"

You will never find time to do anything that doesn't require survival. Instead, you make the time.

I recommend going to Groupon, Living Social or KGB Deals, grabbing a business friend (not your girlfriend or wife unless she happens to be your business partner), and booking a 2 night stay anywhere that has self contained facilities. As long as it has a lounge and a restaurant it's fine. Be prepared to work the entire weekend and don't go with the intention of chilling out. When I go to these places I dial up the intensity so much, it's borderline unhealthy. Just keep working non-stop.

I'll let you in on a little secret. I actually wrote the majority of this book during one of these weekends. I'm currently averaging 10,000 words a day. Your emails should be about 200-300 words each. Don't try telling me you can't write 17 emails, at around 5000 words, in the space of a weekend. That's easy if you know your subject.

Schedule Them In Advance

Using an online email marketing service like MailChimp (see Chapter 4), simply schedule all these emails at the dates you'll decide shortly. The help system within MailChimp is super helpful. I'm a big advocate - it's a great service.

When To Send Emails?

I always schedule my emails that are delivering information on Tuesdays, Wednesdays or Thursdays at mid-morning (11:00am) and any that require action at mid-afternoon (3:00pm). Follow this advice if you want people to actually read your emails: Always use their first name in the subject line and include a subtle but decent reminder to buy things from you. You can even include an emoji to stand out in the inbox.

Once you do this, you can more or less relax for the entire year in terms of your marketing. Of course there will be things you hadn't planned for which you'll need to work on and factor in, but at least you know that if you did nothing else; you would have a decent marketing effort going out to your email list.

Planning Your Email Content

What I want you to do now is think about some of the content you can send out. Come up with some ideas on a separate sheet of paper then, once you have a rough plan, use the next 2 pages to plan it out. I've left 4 spaces per month because you don't really want to be doing more than 1 email a week. Obviously if you think that's too much then scale it back. If you do nothing else, start with one every 3 weeks. It keeps it irregular and at odd times in the month. I know it sounds backwards but this will help your emails stand out.

One thing people often get overwhelmed with, and it's a total overreaction, is thinking they need to come up with different content for their email marketing, direct mail, social media and blog. It's nonsense. You can "recycle" your content and use the same writing in blog posts, videos, social media - everything. Just put the same content out in different formats.

Your appearance in these different mediums should all align. If you've written a new blog post or sent an email, it should be apparent from your Twitter, FaceBook, LinkedIn, Email Campaigns and your Blog. Remember, not everyone is going to follow you on all these sites, they might only read your emails and follow you on Twitter so post all updates everywhere.

Right now, spend a few moments thinking about the kind of content and emails you'd like to send to your list over the next 12 months. Start from wherever we are in the year and either run to the end of the year, or do the full 12 months. It's up to you.

MARKETING CALENDAR

Month 1:

Month 2:

Month 3:

MARKETING CALENDAR

Month 4:

_____

_____

_____

_____

Month 5:

_____

_____

_____

_____

Month 6:

_____

_____

_____

_____

MARKETING CALENDAR

Month 7:

Month 8:

Month 9:

MARKETING CALENDAR

Month 10:

Month 11:

Month 12:

DIFFERENT TYPES OF
EMAIL MARKETING

One of the best ways to make sure that your marketing is handled is to set up an automated email marketing campaign. I want to explain something here - there are two ways you can do this: The first I've already mentioned in the 'Annual Marketing Calendar' section, which is writing and scheduling an email in advance, to be delivered to whoever happens to be on your list at the time when it's sent. The second way to do this is with what's called an autoresponder. This is where you create a set sequence of pre-written emails which will be emailed to each new subscriber who signs up to your list. The difference is that they each get 'email 1' a set number of days after they subscribe, then 'email 2' a set number of days after that and so on. Each new subscriber gets the same experience regardless of when they join the list.

CREATING YOUR OWN
AUTORESPONDERS

The best use of an autoresponder is for education marketing. We use them because we have a complicated product which people need to 'come around to' over time. They don't know they need us right away because we aren't a commodity business like a plumber or a web design company. Even if you are a commodity business, autoresponders can be great for keeping in contact with useful tips. Even someone like a plumber or lawyer could use them to great effect. They're very much an 'as you need it' type of purchase, but both examples could easily put together a 'once a month' autoresponder to begin once someone's come in contact, or after a sale. It'll 'keep them warm' and keep you in the front of your client's mind until they're ready to buy again.

When should I use an Autoresponder?

There are generally two points at which you could use them:

- On the back of some content marketing
- When someone has bought from you.

You'll find if you have a short sales process then you'll be better off with one starting after the purchase. If you have a long, drawn out sales process then starting it when someone comes in contact with you, and using it to convince someone to do business with you will work best. Of course there would be nothing wrong with having a different one start once they're working with you too.

How We Use Autoresponders

In our business, we use a multitude of different autoresponders. The most effective one is once someone has signed up to Better Proposals. This is a 3-month auto responder that gets less and less frequent as time goes on. We do this because someone's interest levels are much higher at the beginning and are more tolerant of frequent email. If it goes past 2 months and they haven't engaged us properly then we're really trying to win them back at that point.

We start off with the Better Proposals autoresponder by reminding them of the things the software will help them do. We start with the most impressive things first and work backwards. We don't pretend they are personal emails, it's pretty clear they're automated but because they are useful, timely tips about software they have just signed up for, they don't mind. We always time our autoresponders to go out at 10:30am. Over time, we've tested this and have found 10:30am and 3:00pm to be the best times to send these kinds of emails.

You might be wondering why I'm suggesting sending autoresponders at 10:30am when 8 pages ago I said to send emails at 11:00am. The reason for this, is you'll know when you've scheduled emails. You'll forget about your autoresponders. If you set them both for 11:00am, you'll find some people getting bombarded. The 30-minute gap is enough to give them a breather if you do end up catching them on the same day.

The key to any great autoresponder campaign is to educate your readers and bring them round to a single way of thinking. An autoresponder with no clear call to action is a waste. In addition, don't sell too early. In the autoresponders for my other book, Cocktails & Palm Trees, we don't even try and sell until about month four. You might be thinking "Month four! How long IS that thing?!". About a year. :-)

Be patient, but timely. Start asking for the sale at a logical time.

What Software Do I Need To Do This

We use MailChimp, and I recommend you do the same. Read my review in Chapter 4 to find out more about it. There are plenty of other apps out there that will do the same thing but frankly, I've tested most of them and they're overly complicated and not that great. Apart from anything else, MailChimp have the best free plan ever. When you create your account, go to the help section and just watch how to set up the autoresponders. There's no point me explaining it, as their software might have been updated by the time this is published and they'll do a far better job than I will.

LEAD MAGNETS AND
MARKETING FUNNELS

What is a lead magnet and marketing funnel?

The holy grail of marketing is having people sign up to something called a "marketing funnel" which drops nearly fully qualified leads right into your inbox. For this you need what's called a lead magnet, which is simply a piece of content which you give away in exchange for contact details. This isn't a new concept but it's crazy how businesses could take advantage of this and don't. A good example of a great lead magnet is this book. This is the revised version and the original has been out for around 4 years. The tools I used:

- Two weekends away to write it - £800 tops
- Lulu.com to print it - £4 each roughly
- MailChimp to capture the contact details of the leads and send the automatic emails - Was still on the free account
- Printed.com to make a nice 'Congratulations' card - 8p each
- Some envelopes off eBay - £13 for 100

In total it took less than a month of writing and editing (…and a lifetime of learning) and hard costs of around £1,000. This has produced at least £250,000 over the last 4 years. Do I have your attention now?

How to create a Marketing Funnel

Because of our web experience, we custom created our marketing funnels depending on what they need to do. We recommend asking your web designer for the options available to you. If you are a customer of ours or are planning on trialling our software, get in touch, because we can advise your web designer on how to connect your lead page to your website. This will mean that any new signups to your lead magnet will go straight into your CRM system. What's better than that, you can also have a "tracking code" captured so you can see exactly which ads are working.

If you can use Wordpress, you can go to something like ThemeForest.net and download a lead capture theme for about £15. Within minutes you can have it set up and ready to collect leads.

Delivering the Lead Magnet

Obviously, you want your new lead to receive your lead magnet, be it a download, a video, a book or whatever but the whole reason you are doing this is to ensure they start to get your emails. You need to play on when they are at their most motivated. The trick is to put the download, or whatever it is in that first email. Do not make the mistake of putting the link on the 'thank you' page. We actually did this and found that over 20% IMMEDIATELY unsubscribed. They got what they were after and weren't about to sit around receiving emails.

Advanced: REAL Marketing Automation

MailChimp has really stepped its email automation game up in the last year. What I'm about to describe to you is only part of their paid plan but seeing as their paid plans start at about £8 per month, it's hardly a huge expense. Most service businesses don't sell just one single thing. There's usually a theme of different services. A web designer might sell new websites, website optimisation, branding and SEO services.

Your lead magnet is typically going to be focused on one specific thing. It might be "8 changes you can make to your homepage to get more leads". That's hyper focused on website optimisation. That's awesome but it hasn't really helped you get a lead for SEO. Of course, you'll run a similar campaign for the SEO side of the business but isn't it possible that the guy that wanted more leads in the first campaign might be interested in your SEO services? This is where MailChimp's clever 'click triggers' come into play.

What it allows you to do is send a series of emails about website optimisation but send one that bridges the gap between that and SEO just slightly. Then when you tell the user to click through to your website or blog or whatever your call to action is, MailChimp will automatically start the auto responder for SEO too. If you have 5-10 different sectors you operate in and you're constantly cross selling between them, you can start to get yourself a seriously powerful marketing machine going.

That kind of technology for less than £10 a month - incredible.

So that's all nice and fancy, lots of cool landing pages with lead magnets on and wonderful autoresponders but what about traffic?

Pay Per Click is Your Friend

Some people swear by it, others curse it. Personally, I'm a fan. This book isn't about debating marketing methods so I'll just detail what I've found to work really well and let you make your own mind up. I'm not going to tell you how to "do PPC". This is just a quick opinion.

LinkedIn Advertising

I would highly recommend looking at LinkedIn Advertising if you sell to business owners and you have a sensible profit margin. By sensible, I mean at least £1,000. LinkedIn Advertising is not cheap by any stretch but it's well worth it. A little cheat is to sign up in USD because it ends up cheaper if you're in the UK.

Cost: Expensive

Lead quality: Excellent

Twitter Ads

Why more people aren't using this is honestly shocking. It's the closest thing to daylight robbery I can think of. Let me set the scene, you can do the internet equivalent of standing outside your competitor's shop and poaching their customers. Technically what you do is run a specific ad for all followers of a certain Twitter user. Of course, that Twitter user is your competition with a much bigger audience than you have.

Cost: Cheap

Lead quality: Good

Facebook Ads

I have mixed opinions about Facebook Ads. It is quite clearly capable of producing some unbelievable results, I just haven't managed to get a lot from it. It's pretty hard to target business owners of certain sectors. If we're being honest, "business owners" who sit on Facebook clicking on ads often turn out to be, what we call, wantrepreneurs - people who sit at home pretending to have a business or wanting to start one, but never actually doing it. They will tick all the boxes of a business owner from a targeting perspective but will often have no customers and no need for your product.

Cost: Cheap

Lead quality: Poor

Google Adwords

If you are going to do this, do it under the guidance of a professional and give them a sensible amount of money to play with. Do not do "content marketing" with Google Adwords - it will suck money up. If you are going to do it, use keywords that imply they are buying not looking. It can work unbelievably well, it's just not as forgiving on the wallet as some of the others.

Cost: Expensive

Lead quality: Good

AUTOMATING
SOCIAL MEDIA... OR NOT?

Should you automate social media?

I do not think so. I think announcements can be automated, like blog posts or content being pushed to your site that you'd like to let your followers know about. That said, if you use Twitter, Facebook and Instagram as your primary tools, how long is it going to take you to log into those services and post them.

The social media game changes so much, it's nearly impossible to keep up with the new ways people are ranking things these days, but here are things that have changed recently:

- Twitter prioritises posts with images
- Facebook hates you sharing from tools like Hootsuite so it buries your content
- Sharing a YouTube video to your Facebook page is pointless, less than 10% of people will see it. Uploading it directly will be rewarded by Facebook's algorithm.

Almost none of these things were in effect 6 months ago but if one thing is clear, it's that you can't very well automate these platforms and still use them properly. They aren't distribution tools, they are engagement tools.

My opinion is that if you want to use social media, then actually use it. Don't get third party tools to post things for you just to save you a few minutes. Schedule it in your calendar and book in a time to post your content at a time when it makes sense.

SUMMARY
OF CHAPTER 5

Automating your marketing is simply about writing the **right content**, then using the **right technology** to get it to the **right people.**

None of this is new technology, in fact it's almost considered standard these days. Remember, no incredible system will make up for awful content. Your message still needs to be good, your copy still needs to be convincing and your offer still needs to be solid. Without those components, you'll have a fancy marketing system with no-one to talk to.

I recommend taking time out and planning this in a hotel over a weekend. Concentrate on writing a series of autoresponders or an Annual Marketing Calendar as a holistic marketing piece split into sections, delivered over a period of time. This is more effective than writing sporadically where there's no connection, no story, and it's just incoherent rambling.

So, all of this marketing activity is going to generate leads for you. Now let's move onto looking at how you can use some of the technology I mentioned in Chapter 4 to Automate Your Sales.

Chapter 6

Automate Your Sales

"Here's how you sell. You say, here's what I've got, this is what it'll do for you and this is what I want you to do next. It's that simple"

Frank Kern - Internet Marketer

HOW DO YOU AUTOMATE SELLING?

Something I notice very quickly whenever dealing with any business is their complete lack of a sales process. It's not a dig at them; hardly any of us have one. It seems we've got confused between having a sales process and simply being really good at making it up as we go along. I think this comes from being the business owner and not having a "boss" of some kind to enforce a sales procedure. If there's one thing you should have learned in this book so far is that you can't automate a non-existent process.

"But it's only me doing it"

It's a valid argument that, if you're the only person selling the services, why do you need a process? The answer lies in the experience the customer has. When you're selling, the idea is to guide them through your process. I don't believe in pushy sales but if someone wants to buy something from you, they shouldn't feel like they need to discover what the next step is themselves. In all of our proposals (and I recommend you do the same) is a 'Next Step' section. Here's what ours looks like:

1. Ask any questions you might have, then when you're ready, sign the proposal by typing your name in the box below and hitting 'Sign Proposal'.
2. After that, I'll be in touch to arrange our Setup Interview.
3. We'll then set your system up and import your data.
4. Launch Week will consist of over the phone training and integrating your website with your Business Automation CRM.

People have enough to worry about when buying something new. This only gets worse the more expensive and complicated the product is. What I've done here is try to alleviate their concerns by explaining the entire process to our potential new customer. The last thing they need is having to figure things out. When designing your sales process and documenting it, which we're about to do shortly, make sure you follow these two rules:

Rule 1: Make it clear

The most important thing is to make it clear upfront what is going to happen. Why is bungee jumping scary? It's the "what if?" factor. Try and remove that by explaining each stage and what's expected of them.

Rule 2: Make it simple

There are so many business owners I've met who complicate the hell out of the simple idea of exchanging money for a service, it's unbelievable. I have a client who used to get his POTENTIAL clients to sign a Non-Disclosure Agreement before even talking to them!

It's madness! The first thing he's saying to people is "Hi, I don't trust you, and just to show you that, I'm going to make you jump through this ridiculous hoop of signing and scanning this 8 page document."

Please don't do this. It's bad for your bank account. The idea is to keep things as simple as they can possibly be. It should be as seamless as buying a beer from a bar. There's no complication there. You give them some money, they give you beer. You are happy and so are they. Let's take that same approach to your sales process and see how simple we can make it.

What we'll do in a moment is work out exactly what your sales process is, then we'll try to eliminate parts and simplify it.

LET'S WORK OUT YOUR CURRENT SALES PROCESS

It's really quite simple. Just write down everything that happens from the initial contact through to the deal being signed and everything that happens in between. What do you respond with if there's any negotiation? How do you set up a sales meeting? Do you ask questions in order to make a proposal? How do you ask for the business? - an email, a phone call, an online demo, a meeting? What happens when they say yes? How do they approve that proposal? How do you invoice them? How do they pay? What happens next?

As an example, here's ours:

1. They respond to our marketing by showing interest in a discovery process or by signing up for a trial.

2. I ask a lot of specific questions at this stage to find out about their business. I will know at this point if I'm putting a proposal together for a custom system, one of our off-the-shelf products or if we can't help at all.

3. I produce the proposal or send a "Sorry we couldn't help" email.

4. They sign the proposal electronically and receive our 'New Customer' form which allows us to collect billing details etc. This automatically gets fed back into our CRM.

5. They set up their Direct Debit mandate with GoCardless.

At each stage, I pre-empt the next step by talking about it a little bit and making sure they are comfortable each step of the way. With our kind of sale, there's lots of unknown bits to consider so a little more education is a nice touch. You adapt it to suit your style though.

Okay, so now you've got an idea for it, let's do it!

On the next page, write down every single step that someone goes through to do business with you. From initial enquiry (however that happens) right up to someone giving you money. We'll deal with what happens after later in the book.

YOUR CURRENT SALES PROCESS

Alright great stuff and well done! What I'll do is explain some common ways I have figured out over the years, for simplifying some of the steps. Usually when I'm working with private clients, I find I can get rid of several stages immediately using these three methods. Without seeing what you've just written, that's going to be slightly difficult so if you email me a picture of the previous page to adam@businessautomation.co.uk I'll give you my thoughts on it.

Here are three tried and tested ways of improving almost any sales process:

Method 1: How quickly can you ask for the business?

Try to figure out what they want as quickly as possible. If it's a really consultative process then you might need several phone calls or meetings to make this happen. The sooner you say "Would you like us to work with you on this?", the sooner they can give you reasons why not, and the sooner you can overcome those issues and move forward with helping them out.

Method 2: Merge steps where possible

If, for example you ask your new client to send you some information and you later ask for billing details, you can probably merge those two steps. Any time where you are asking your client for information, try and do all that in one go. Anytime you they need to get them to sign anything, do that in one go too. You get the picture.

Method 3: Capture details electronically

If you take down their details, instead of doing this over the phone or in an email, get them to do it by sending them a link to a nicely designed form on your website that is linked to your CRM system. There's less margin for error, they feel in control and it's less work for you.

Method 4: Send a proposal and get it signed electronically

Always be sending a proposal. Even if you are a print company quoting someone £50 for some business cards, you should have a template ready to go and send them a proposal. This gives you and them something to base the sale on, it formalises the particulars (price, delivery date, specification and payment terms). In addition, making them sign it online speeds up the sale.

WORKING OUT
WHAT YOUR PROSPECTS WANT

It's all well and good having a fancy sales process, but if when you walk into the meeting or get on the call, you are a like a kid in a candy store then you might as well not bother simplifying your sales process at all. You want to go into any sales environment in a calm, collected manner and do what my friend Jeff likes to call 'executing the programme'. We're going to create that 'programme' for you right now because it's the bit that makes all of this easy.

It's often called a 'Needs Analysis' but I prefer to call it a 'Discovery Process'. This could be a case of asking 1 or 2 questions and then telling someone a price over the phone after 90 seconds, or it could be a 3 month back and forth discussion, ending with a 4 hour discussion in their boardroom. Whatever it is, you want to identify what you need to know as quickly as possible in order to give them your proposal.

In this next exercise, I want you to write down a list of the things you need to ask people in order to put a quote together and create your proposal. If you have a massive set of questions like we do (20-30), then grab a separate sheet of paper. It'll take a matter of minutes and I recommend you do it **now** to get the most out of this section.

If this turns out to be a few questions you can ask on the phone, then print it off and stick it next to the phone. If you meet people in a longer sales process then print it off and stick several copies in your travel bag. This is your 'Discovery Process'.

Someone I've learned a lot from in the past is a great information marketing guy by the name of Eben Pagan. His business does in excess of $30,000,000 a year in sales and he teaches consultants to be more effective when selling. He uses this classic trick:

When you're sitting with the client, ask them all of your questions, write them all down in the space you provide on your sheet then say:

"Just so I understand this correctly, can I read this back to you to make sure we're on the same wavelength?"

Then just read them their answers back, abbreviated. They will be absolutely delighted with you. It sounds so simple it's almost patronising, but so many people don't do this. Most people just leave. Think about how confusing it must be for someone who just spent an hour talking with you and you get up and say, "Okay thanks I'll be in touch soon" and leave. Reading their answers back lets them get excited about the fact that you've clearly understood them.

Using the expertise of someone who clearly has no problem selling products to people, let's try emulating this. If you sell various different products or services, then come up with a set of questions for each one but try to combine them where possible to keep it streamlined.

Remember, this will become your Discovery Process. Whenever you're in front of anyone in a sales situation, use these questions to figure out what they want, then present your proposal and ask for the business. It's really no more complicated than that.

YOUR DISCOVERY PROCESS

YOUR DISCOVERY PROCESS

QUOTES AND PROPOSALS

Send Everyone a Proposal

Sending a proposal to a prospect is not a special occasion. It's a regular way of doing business, which you must adopt. Every sale you make should be done with a proposal with absolutely zero exceptions. There are so many reasons for this but I'll give you the top few.

It forms a contract:

Every business has the need to protect themselves. Do you have a basic contract that covers you in all eventualities? Could you imagine us, as a CRM company not having a provision in our contract that says we can't be sued through loss of data.

Formalises the deal:

Have you ever had someone verbally agree to do business with you, then pull out for some reason? We all have. That is probably because you gave them nothing to sign. Pulling out after signing should have financial ramifications detailed in the contract or proposal.

"This is how we do things around here"

When you send a proposal, it's your chance to say to your client "This is how we do things around here". It's a chance to show them how much you care about the details, about design, about your subject. It's a chance to tell your story at a time when you have their upmost attention. More importantly, it's a chance to show that you really listened when you went through your Discovery Process with them. It's that listening, then relaying the details that are important to them that gets you the job.

It looks more professional:

When you send someone a proposal, it's a big moment for them. When you receive a proposal, you're usually excited to learn more about a service you're about to buy. Don't disappoint them by sending a one-liner email or a crappy "Quote Template" you found in Microsoft Word. Speaking of what not to send, let's look at that now.

This is not a proposal

A proposal is a multi-page document which fully demonstrates without doubt that you are the only company that they should consider choosing. A proposal is not:

- An email with a 2 line description
- A standard PDF with basic information attached to an email with the price.
- A Microsoft Word document that looks like this:

AUTOMATE YOUR BUSINESS

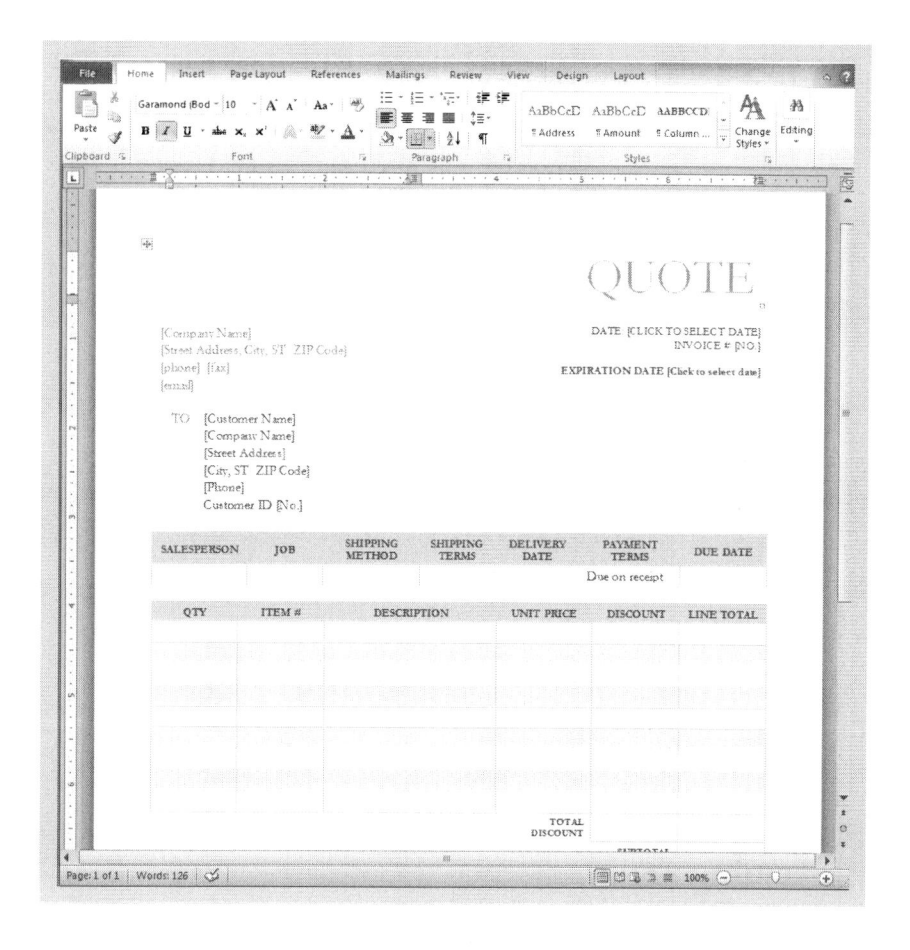

7 things every proposal must include

On our YouTube Channel, I uploaded a video which I recorded in Les Deux-Alpes in France which detailed the 7 things you must include in any proposal. Here they are:

1. Executive Summary or Introduction:

State the problem they are having, and the solution you're going to provide.

2. Full description:

This serves two purposes, the first is so you know what you're doing and the client knows what they're getting. The second is that is actually forms the basis of a contract.

3. Case study:

Get a case study that is relevant to that particular client. Ideally, this should be from an existing client from a similar industry or job.

4. Things you do that your competition don't:

Every business does things that their competition don't. These are the little things you do because you know they need to be done but you can't really charge for them. Think of them and put them here.

5. Price:

Include a summary on the price page of all the benefits of choosing you.

6. Guarantee:

If you don't have one, make one up. Money back guarantee is a simple enough 'go-to' one that everyone understands.

7. Terms and Conditions:

Include your contract here. Don't wait until they verbally say yes, THEN send the contract. Just include it in the proposal.

How to template your proposals

Dedicating time:

The first thing is to actually dedicate some time to writing your proposal template. It should include all 7 things I mentioned in the previous section. I personally like removing myself from phones and the grind and really getting my head into it. I've mentioned this before, but even just going to a smart hotel for the day helps to block the time out. You don't have to move - just sit there and order whatever you need, whenever you want it. So long as you get your work done, it'll be money well spent. You might find an office or your home an inspiring place to write. I do, but not as much as a new surrounding.

Where to start from:

It's important to remember not to just use the last proposal you sent as a template. When it comes to creating your template, you can use what you've sent someone before as a starting point but be prepared to strip it away and re-write it if need be.

Product proposal, not company proposal

Create a proposal for the service you are selling, not for your company. Yes, you should have a little bit in there about your company and it should have strong company branding but remember what your prospect is buying. It's about the work you've done in the past, not how long you've been in business. There are three levels to your proposals. There's the company level, then the product or service level, then there's the client level. Keep that in mind.

FOLLOW UP WITH ENQUIRIES
LIKE A SALES NINJA

Following up with sales enquiries is the task we wish we all did more of but never have the time for. We know how effective it is and we certainly appreciate it when people do it to us, so why do we find it so hard?

I know that in our business I used to be the world's worst at following up with people I'd sent a proposal to. I conducted some research amongst some of our clients and I certainly wasn't alone, so I dug deeper. Here's what I found:

- They were certain they'd make more money if they followed up more.
- They didn't because they didn't have the time.
- The reason they didn't have the time was because they felt each email needed to be written from scratch.
- They had no quick way of reminding themselves to contact the person.

So a follow up system that pre-empts what you want to say, reminds you when to do it and takes almost no time would be a pretty good start! We looked around and found nothing that solved all these issues at once, so we decided to make something ourselves and start using it internally.

Immediately I noticed that I was being reminded to contact people that I knew I had completely forgotten about. This happened again and again so I knew we were on to something.

CREATING YOUR OWN FOLLOW UP SYSTEM

Different Sequences

Depending on your sales process, you'll need different sequences to cater for the different stages your enquiries can be at. We use three:

1. Pre-Proposal - Personal emails to go alongside our autoresponders.
2. Post-Proposal - Getting them to sign their proposal.
3. Post-Launch - Standard after-sales care. Making sure they're okay.

My suggestion is to just focus on implementing one follow up sequence to start with. I would choose either Pre-Proposal or Post-Proposal. To find out which one you would benefit from the most, just look at the biggest drop off rate in your sales process. If most people you speak to want a proposal, then that area of your business doesn't have much of an issue and you should focus on Post-Proposal to increase conversion. If on the other hand your conversion rate is fairly good but you could do with sending more proposals, then focus on a Pre-Proposal sequence.

What to Say and When to Say it?

This completely depends on your business, what you sell, how you sell it and a million other factors but I can tell you that you already have a near perfect working template, you just aren't using it.

Go through your inbox and sent items and find the last sale you made where you had to chase. Look at the emails you sent and mark out the key ones where you were pro-active. Those are the emails that are going to make up the content. Also, look at the timing of the emails you sent and that will dictate the time delay between each communication. Were you leaving it quite a long time between emails? Be honest with yourself, could you maybe have sped up the process by being a little more aggressive in terms of timing?

I have made a spreadsheet which you can download below. It has some sample messages, the timing and a little marker for who's received which email. If you have a small number of sales enquiries and clients and you are good at keeping spreadsheets up to date then it'll be fine. Ask yourself this though, if you are forgetting to follow up, are you going to remember to update this spreadsheet?

Follow Up System Spreadsheet:

https://www.businessautomation.co.uk/downloads/followup-spreadsheet

SUMMARY
OF CHAPTER 6

Automating your sales process as best you can will make an absolutely huge difference to your revenue and stress levels.

Making everything electronic removes margin for error and speeds things up, allowing you to strike while the iron is hot.

Having a set of questions known as a Discovery Process allows you to get other people to carry out your sales in your absence or create a standard way for people in your business to sell or if nothing else, make it easier for yourself.

Sending world-class proposals not only helps you win the job, but also helps you get that job quicker and with less time invested in creating it. Now once you've sent that proposal, you've got a superb follow-up system which you can use to systemise your follow-up activity and win jobs you would have otherwise forgotten about.

Keeping things simple is the key to an automated sales process. But what next? You've got the order, now what? It's time to automate your workflow.

Chapter 7

Automate Your Workflow

"**Your company's most valuable asset is how it is known to its customers**"

Brian Tracy - Success Coach

AUTOMATING YOUR
WORKFLOW

Automating your sales process is all well and good but if your workflow or the "getting it done" part is a total mess, then the whole show is going to fall apart the second you sell anyone anything. Why can I say this with confidence? I experienced exactly this with a branch of Prontaprint I'll tell you about shortly.

Think about it this way; when you buy something, you really expect everything to appear simple, smooth and to feel like you're part of some sort of process. When you come across a company with scattered operations, it's hard to trust them.

If you never know when anything's going to be done, your customers don't know who to contact and everyone's left trying to figure out what's going on, it's pretty tricky to have faith in your service. This means that customers are unlikely to refer you as much, even if the end product is pretty solid. This is vital to growing your business! Try to make your customer's experience of dealing with you so good, that they want others they know to get the same experience. You must gear your processes up with referrals in mind. I find that the easiest way to have your customers feel at ease with you, is simply explain everything during the sales process, then re-state it once they agree to do business with you.

Explain timescales and the process upfront

It's so easy to do, yet people seem to think that it's okay to just sell something to someone then forget all about them. Please, let's try to give these people at least some hope of knowing what's going to happen next. Experience has taught me my clients love this level and type of service. The way I like to do this is put the key stages in the proposal but you could just as easily make it a page on your website with examples and timescales to really let people into the 'behind the scenes' workings of your process.

For instance, if you agree a date with someone for an installation or meeting of some sort, I find the best way to let people know what's happening is to send a specially designed PDF. This feels unique and specific for them, so they'll read it. Here's an example: The director of a flooring company we work with, was telling me that occasionally the client leaves the room filled with stuff. This makes their work a nightmare before they've even started. The reason this probably happens is because they're not telling them separately. 90% of their communication will take place over the phone or in person, so telling them in amongst all the other chat - they're bound to forget. What about if they did this:

Once they signed the agreement with the fitting date and their Terms and Conditions, they sent them a PDF confirming the date of fitting and under an 'Everything you need to do' section, detail the customer's part of the deal and lay out the consequences for not adhering to this (delays, extra charges etc). This is also another opportunity to communicate with them, ask for referrals and generally have them think good of you. In the process of sorting out an everyday problem, so the fitters can be more productive, they have also been absolutely clear about what's happening next. This keeps the customer delighted because there are "no surprises". It looks like you're really putting them first.

Once the customer is happy, the next problem occurs - internal communication. If you have a team of three or four working in some sort of production line, you might have experienced the problem of one person doing their part of the job, then not being concerned with the rest of the project. Not only does this not give that staff member a holistic view of the end product, but what happens if the customer calls to ask how it's coming along? Either the person who answers has to admit they have no idea or go pestering people to find out. Neither looks good to the customer. Let's look at the ideal scenario and try to model that instead.

What You Want

Ideally you want to have the ability for anyone in the business to check and know exactly what stage each job is at, at any point in time. In order to do that, we need to work out exactly what your production process is. For some of you, this will be really easy. In some cases, when you sell different services or products, you might need to produce a few different ones if the processes are different.

Your Workflow Process

The first thing you really need to do is to think about the different milestones that each job goes through. Start this from when the customer has agreed to do business with you, and end when you've finished the job. For example, our custom Business Automation System projects go like this:

1. Planning meeting
2. Design the layout of the software
3. Project Manager writes instructions and technical specification
4. Allocate developers for certain sections
5. Test the work when it's finished
6. Deal with any final snags
7. Launch and final test

It's not overly complicated but it's necessary to know. The "doing the work" bit is where you spend most your time, and this gives it some actual structure. When you've done this exercise and you operate by it, you'll realise that certain parts can be systemised and made easier. For instance, the passing of information from one staff member to another, how is this currently done? A meeting? A phone call? An email? A chat by the water cooler? Even those awful Post-It notes?

My advice would be to always try to remove meetings where possible. Our Head Developer, Grace works from her home in Sao Paolo, Brazil, whilst I could be based at home, a ski lift, or the top of the Empire State Building. This means we all end up doing a lot of our work communicating in Basecamp, which keeps it regimented and mistake-free because it's a single line of communication.

Make a list now of the order your production process happens in. Try and break it down like my example instead of just putting "sell it, do the work, invoice it".

YOUR WORKFLOW

EXAMPLE:
DON'T DO THIS

As I'm writing this, I'm sitting with someone now who has a supplier they work with who made one massive and embarrassing mistake! They sent the client a letter containing confidential information to what they thought was his address, but got the house number wrong. Worse than that, the person who received the letter was a competitor who promptly stole the business! This occurred because of an error in **writing something down** and that is the key problem. In today's world where everything is electronic, why are we manually transcribing information like contact details? It's utter madness!

What we all need to do is try wherever possible to remove human interaction when it comes to repetitive processes. This removes the potential for error and keeps people focused on doing what they're great at instead of making them do admin work they're not interested in.

My guess is that everyone's least favourite thing about their job would probably be "paperwork". Let's do what we're best at and let the computers do the admin stuff in future.

Here's an example of exactly what not to do. I dealt with a major franchise printing company in Hove recently (Prontaprint) and this was my experience:

I spoke to the manager who was a convincing enough salesman and sold me some business cards and pull-up banners for one of our events. He passed me over to his designer who sent me some mock-ups via email. I was always a bit nervous over the cost because I had no idea if the design was a set cost or if it was an hourly rate. After some back and forth, we eventually came to a design I liked. Once I'd signed it off by having to print off a sheet of paper, sign it then scan it and send it back, they went completely silent. I called up a few weeks later to find out what was going on and no-one had any idea and couldn't seem to call me back and let me know. I was passing by their shop four days later and thought I'd just call in, and sure enough - there's my banner in the front of the office and my boxes of cards sitting on the floor. I ask the designer how no-one knew where my stuff was, he told me it had been there over a week. Bit weird. He designed it and he'd walked past it probably 30 times in that week and didn't think to call me? Shocking!

Here's what they should have done:

Have a simple spreadsheet on Google Docs so multiple people can edit it at once then lay it out like this:

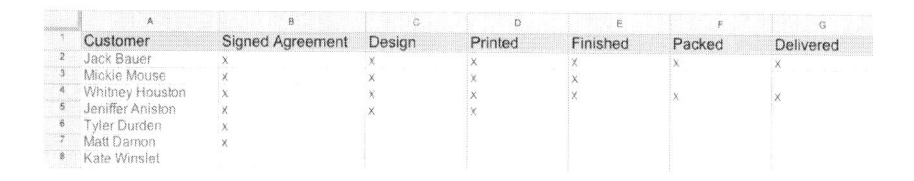

	A	B	C	D	E	F	G
1	Customer	Signed Agreement	Design	Printed	Finished	Packed	Delivered
2	Jack Bauer	x	x	x	x	x	x
3	Mickie Mouse	x	x	x	x		
4	Whitney Houston	x	x	x	x	x	x
5	Jeniffer Aniston	x	x	x			
6	Tyler Durden	x					
7	Matt Damon	x					
8	Kate Winslet						

With the customers down the left and across the top all the different milestones of production. Then every time the designer completes his bit for example, he puts a mark in his section against that job, then emails the files to the next person. Not only is this more organised internally but when a client calls up and says "Any idea how my job is coming along?" someone can look at that spreadsheet in a matter of seconds and give a really accurate description of where the job is and how long it'll take to finish.

Imagine my example, if I'd called up and asked, and the designer said "Oh yeah it's actually in packing now which means it'll probably be ready tomorrow. Is that cool?" How much better is that? It's better organised internally which gives you confidence in what you're doing day to day, and in turn makes you look like business rockstars to your customers. How long will it take to set this up? Maybe 5 minutes?

So, that's how you could use a simple spreadsheet to keep track of your production process. What about if you are using Basecamp or an online To-Do List app? In Basecamp you can create a project for each client, so when you sell something to someone, you simply add the stages to a To-Do List and assign them to the correct people. This will send them an email with the details of the task. This makes the product better, the customer happier and keeps everyone involved.

The benefit of doing this is massive. It keeps the entire managerial role almost non-existent which is perfect, so everyone can do what they're best at. This is something I think businesses miss these days. Instead of hiring a single person to do a single job amazingly, they hire multi-taskers and jack-of-all-trades types because everyone needs to chip in and help around the office and do generic tasks.

It's really a bizarre situation because clearly it's not the amount of time it takes to set these things up that stops people from doing it. It could be fear of getting it wrong or maybe business owners today just aren't bothered about having a streamlined business. If you're planning on growing your business you need to create more time for yourself – how are you planning to do that? Have we all come to the point where we want the stresses of business but don't want to enjoy the lifestyle that goes with it? What's wrong with us? Hopefully by writing this book I can open people's eyes to the idea of putting systems in place and enjoying life a bit more.

As I've said previously, my dream is to build my own home using nothing but my friends to do it. I'm never going to be able to pull that off if I'm required to be working 60 hour weeks just to keep the business ticking over. The way I'm going to do that, and you're welcome to emulate my path which was discovered through years of trial and error, is by using systems to do my work for me while I, the **business person**, focus on doing just that, generating **business**.

I have a belief that the idea of an "admin assistant" will soon be gone. In time, people will use software to replace "admin people" and instead only hire people with technical skills to actually increase sales or increase production. Everything else should be taken care of by a system which will grow happily as your revenue and production team grows.

The Ideal Situation

I want you to think about something for a moment. What if, instead of having a spreadsheet or an off the shelf system, you had an experience which made your business appear so simple to your customers, it was a selling point in itself? What if it made your staff's jobs so much easier they actually enjoyed work more? What if above all else, it removed you from the system so you became what you should be: A business owner? This is what we've been doing successfully for years for a whole range of different businesses. Let me demonstrate how this *could* work.

Let's stick with our printing company example for a moment and just imagine...

Sales:

A lead comes in via the phone, and you ask a few questions from your 'Discovery Process' to work out if you can help. You decide you can, so you ask a more detailed set of questions in order to produce their quote. Using your pre-written quote template, make a few modifications to suit your prospect and send it using Better Proposals (remember, we reviewed this in Chapter 4) which the customer signs online. You get an email moments later notifying you that they've signed it. It automatically sends an email to the designer letting him know what to do.

Production:

Once your designer has communicated with the client and had them electronically sign off the artwork, it's immediately sent to the print team who will print the job. They mark it as complete and send it to the finishing/packing team, and once they're done and mark it as complete the clever bit happens. It would send an email to the client explaining it's ready to collect or that it's being dispatched (whatever was agreed when they signed the agreement). It would also automatically invoice them in accordance with the amount you put in when you created the proposal.

After-sales care:

It would then put them into a series of automated emails which would start with one three days later saying "Are you happy with your order, is everything okay?" It would then go on to re-market to this person and sell them more cool stuff. After all, your new customer probably doesn't know all the things you can do for them. Now they know you are a great company, you just need to put the right product in front of them.

All your work files in one place

One of the things that makes a process like this possible is having all the files you need to do your work in one single place. If you do run a print, video production or any type of company dealing with large files, I'd recommend having a central server (backed up of course).

If you run any other type of business like a web design business or a marketing company or anything else, then get Dropbox working for you. Get a good folder structure going and copy everything to Dropbox. It really doesn't matter if you can't do it on the free account. Don't skimp, the files you work with are vital and can't be messed with. Handle this stuff with care.

Make your process your USP

What's the ripple effect of this? It's a service not being provided by anyone else, so your customers rave about how unbelievable you are. The amazing thing is, that's not even the best bit. Think about it, read the scenario again if you like. What work did the business owner actually do? Answered the phone, put the proposal together and sent it using Better Proposals. Everything else was automatic. He could easily outsource that if he wanted.

This is just touching the tip of the iceberg. These systems don't just improve the immediate issues, they often have a massive ripple effect which can very often change the landscape of an entire organisation. This is truly something that allows a small business to have an approach which focuses on revenue and can use its limited resources to compete with bigger businesses.

Think of your processes like a factory

You could be reading this as a freelancer who does everything from marketing to selling, the work itself, billing and support or as a business owner with 40 staff and teams for each of these departments. Whatever your situation, I want you to start thinking of your business as a factory. Really imagine it as a production line. When you start to think of it in this way, you start to adopt some of the traits that make production lines so unbelievably efficient. You could do worse than reading some of Peter Drucker's work - a brilliant mind when it came to management and innovation.

When you think of your business like a factory, you start to look at everything as a process. Which processes are efficient? Which ones are slowing the process down? Only then can you start to answer some of these questions and begin to make improvements to your processes and your business in general.

SUMMARY
OF CHAPTER 7

In this chapter, we've looked at working out what processes you go through on a daily basis to "do the work". We've looked at how you can streamline some of those processes within your business, and how you can use various pieces of web software to simplify them even further.

You could take the exercise in this chapter and repeat it for all the other processes in your business like ordering, hiring, shipping, production and anything else you can apply it to.

Remember, the more simplified your systems are, the easier your entire life becomes. Getting all your files in one place is going to speed up ad-hoc questions around the office to no end. Thinking of your business as a factory is a surefire way to improve the efficiency of your work, stress levels of your team and ultimately the profitability of your company.

Beyond your production process or operations, what happens next? You need the money, so you invoice people right? Let's take a closer look at how you can automate your finances.

Chapter 8

Automate Your Finances

"I buy expensive suits. They just look cheap on me."

Warren Buffet - One of the richest men of all time

PLAY TO YOUR STRENGTHS

Unless you're a finance person, you should not be doing finance. It's something that needs to happen and you still need to retain financial literacy but you shouldn't be messing about invoicing people, inputting expenses, making graphs, plotting out cash-flow forecasts, doing quarterly VAT returns, chasing money or cashing cheques. This chapter is going to be a short one but it can make an absolutely huge difference if you were to implement my suggestions.

WHAT PAYMENT METHODS SHOULD YOU ACCEPT?

Stop accepting cheques... like... yesterday. Just put a sign on your door, website, invoices, wherever, that says "It's the 21st century, we no longer accept cheques!" I was fully under the impression that they were supposed to be phased out by the end of 2013. That never happened, but let's just pretend it did because they're awful!

The only ad hoc payment methods you should accept should be bank transfers, credit cards or an online payment service like PayPal. That's it. The only exception to this is if you have a shop, in which case, cash is semi-required. The fewer payment methods you accept, the less of a headache your bookkeeping is. Do you know how many we accept from new customers? Two. BACS and Direct Debit using GoCardless for UK customers (and PayPal for EU and US customers). Your finances become so simple with this number of payment methods.

Think how many we could accept:

- BACS
- Cheque
- PayPal
- Google Checkout
- Direct Debit
- Standing Order
- Cash
- Credit Card
- Payment in kind

It would be an absolute nightmare to police all of that. The worst culprit of the lot is standing orders. Here are two examples: One where it's a nightmare and the second is the only reason to ever accept it.

Why Standing Orders Are Evil

Back in the day before we set up our Direct Debit system (I'll talk about that shortly), the only way we could accept regular recurring payments was the subscription service built into PayPal or by Standing Order. Most people get confused with the difference between a Standing Order and Direct Debit. A Direct Debit is where you give a company permission to take money from you in a varying amount on a monthly basis. A Standing Order is where you send pre-determined amounts of money to the company on specific dates. Back in the early days of my web design business, we had one customer paying £30 a month by Standing Order. It was for hosting and some other bits, but at some point in the year he'd cancelled it (probably by accident). Because it wasn't a massive amount of money we completely missed it. We figured it out almost a year later and had to chase him for about £300. Not ideal.

When Standing Orders Are Acceptable

The only acceptable reason to use Standing Orders is when the amount is large enough that you'd miss it pretty quickly if it didn't come in. We have someone paying off a £20,000 system with 10x £2,000 payments. We'd know about it if that didn't come in. That said, with GoCardless, you can take any amount up to £5,000 which almost completely eradicates the need for Standing Orders, even for large ticket items.

Accepting Direct Debits Is Not Scary

Accepting Direct Debits was one of the best moves we've ever made as a business. We use a company called GoCardless. It's free to set up, costs nothing each month, it says 'Business Automation Co' on our client's bank statements - not common apparently. They just charge 1% with a maximum fee of £2 per transaction. It's the best investment we've ever made. Here's an example of how simple it makes things - a client was paying £95 a month for their Business Automation CRM on Direct Debit. They wanted a small addition, which cost £150, so we simply added it on to their next payment.

He was amazed at how efficient it seemed and it made the sale so easy he was delighted to be part of it.

Not only that, but we control the amounts. If someone owes you money, you can technically can just take it. Personally, I've never done this because it seems underhanded but technically you could. As of writing, the limit is £5,000 per month per company (using GoCardless).

If you do have the occasional bad payer, it reduces their delay tactics down to almost no time at all. You're not reliant on a "payment run" or them to actually pay you. They just need to give you permission to take it. If they don't have the funds available, they will likely just tell you to hold off a few days (or something similar). If they have an issue with paying you, then they'll have to address that too. Either way, you force their hand rather than waiting and having to chase for weeks on end.

If you accept regular payments from your clients, I highly recommend looking into it. It's free to sign up, improves your cash flow to no-end and makes you look like a really professional outfit.

OUTSOURCING YOUR BOOKKEEPING

Bookkeeping is one of the easiest things to outsource. If you use an online system like Xero then you shouldn't really need to outsource the invoicing; but sending a virtual assistant (VA) an email saying "Invoice Matt Jones £300 for consultancy, due in 7 days from today" and firing it off is a lot easier than messing about in Microsoft Word making your invoices. Your job as business owner is to set these things up, not necessarily use them day in and day out.

What about expenses? Just an idea, but how about keeping all your receipts in a box, then at the end of each week, take pictures with your phone and email them to your Virtual Assistant and tell them to input them into a system like Xero. All the details are on the invoice/receipt so there's no explanation required on your part. It's easy for them. At the end of the year, give your accountant your Xero login details and tell them to crack on. They'll click three buttons and their calculations are done.

Benefits:

1. Your accounting bill is chopped in half
2. You'll only spend maybe £150 over the year in bookkeeping fees
3. You can access reports at any time by logging in and seeing the financial state of your business.

Three massive benefits! The biggest of course being your reduction in accounting fees. After all, why would you want to pay a qualified accountant £100-300/hour to type up your receipts and add up your invoices? It's a totally ludicrous allocation of your hard earned cash. As you become a bigger business, you want to keep scalable fees like accounting costs to a low amount. The more bookkeeping work they need to do the more expensive your fees will be.

Reporting:

I do think you should, as a business owner, know the basic metrics of your business. Things like:

- Sales last month
- Profit last month
- How many customers you have
- What your conversion rate is
- How many leads come from a particular lead source

These are really basic things that you should know, but without mucking about in finance packages or playing silly buggers in Excel with graphs, how do you go about knowing this information?

Built into every system we build are simple reports that show you at the click of a button everything you need to know about your business. Most systems have so many different reports for different things but that can almost be as confusing as just working it out manually. We thought it would be better for you to simply put the dates in that you want your report for and we'll show you everything.

I do wish more companies would take this approach. It's simple, it's easy and above all else, when you're comparing month-to-month or year-to-year, you can put the reports side-by-side and compare each bit knowing it's worked out the same.

SUMMARY
OF CHAPTER 8

Your finances don't need to be scary. It's a machine - just set the system up, write the rules and outsource it using Freelancer.com or Elance.com. This is more about saving you time, not saving tiny amounts of money here and there. The irony is, a simple finance system will save you money anyway.

Now, we've looked at automating almost your entire business machine; your marketing, sales, workflow and finances. Lastly we need to look at the thing that is going to make all that happen. You. It's time to automate yourself.

Chapter 9

Automate Yourself

"Focus on being productive instead of busy"

Tim Ferriss - The Four Hour Work Week

HOW CAN YOU AUTOMATE
A HUMAN BEING?

The final section on automation is the idea of automating yourself. I'm not sure about you, but I've always felt that if I could duplicate myself then I'd be able to achieve anything so much faster. It would be great! There wouldn't be anything I do now, that this "new person" couldn't do.

Unfortunately, at time of writing, all Scientists have managed to do is clone a sheep and call it Dolly, which I don't think will help us much. Assuming that we can't clone humans - how do we go about doing less work, not hiring new staff and getting more done?

It really comes down to the number of time-consuming activities that you do in your average day. For example: travel, starting and stopping a task, implementing quick and random new ideas you can't stop yourself from working on immediately, interruption, learning new things, YouTube, Facebook, phones, texts, emails are all common culprits and they will suck your time away like there's no tomorrow unless you do something about it.

GETTING OUT OF
MEETINGS AND PHONE CALLS

The most destructive time suckers in any business owner's day are meetings. I happen to enjoy them but I pick and choose them very carefully and they're usually sales related. I don't have pointless meetings and you shouldn't either.

The worst case scenario is having to travel for a meeting. Sitting in a car has to be the biggest waste of time in history. You can't work, write or even think properly. About the only thing you can do is talk on the phone and let's be honest - with signal cutting out every 5 minutes on motorways, it's pretty tricky to have a proper conversation. With that being labelled the worst case, what's the best case? - An email.

It's a bit of a stretch to turn a travelling meeting into an email I know, but all it takes is a little bit of persuasion and it's do-able. I like to think about it this way: You always want, at the very least, to move from whatever the originally suggested point of contact was, to the next least time consuming activity. Here's the order:

Most	Meetings where you travel
	Meetings where you don't
	Phone calls
Least	Email

It's important to know this when trying to get out of a meeting. Let's say someone asks for a meeting. First of all, they've asked for it, so they should travel; but if that isn't enough reason, you just need to give them one. I'd rather buy lunch or dinner and have someone come to me, than spend ages in a car. It's not about the money, it's about protecting your time. Think about it this way - if you know you have to pick up the tab if they come to you, then maybe use that as an incentive to do it on the phone?

Moving Meetings to Phone calls

The thing to understand here is you need to try and get across the point that you don't actually need to have a meeting in order to accomplish the task. What happens a lot of the time is people get all freaked out or overwhelmed and "need" a meeting. The easiest way to fix this is get them to tell you exactly what they want the meeting for. I do this with an email to set a "light agenda", I might send something like this:

"Hi John

I respect your time so can I suggest setting a light agenda. Nothing concrete, but I want to avoid you coming all the way down here only for us to forget half of what we were scheduled to talk about. Can you send me a list of the things you'd like to talk about please and I'll add to it if need be?

Thanks
Adam"

It really doesn't matter how you go about this, but you need to get them to put down a list of things they want to talk about. Once they've done that, just call them, ask them if they have 5 minutes and just talk about the rest of it. Cite being confused about one little bit then just talk about the whole thing. Once you get off the phone, send an email telling them you are glad they're happy and you're both on the same page and there's no need for the meeting now. Nice job, you've just saved yourself some time. I know it sounds flippant but honestly, try it and you'll laugh because it just works.

Getting out of phone calls

This is more or less exactly the same process. Ask for an agenda, but instead of calling them back, just reply under each of their points with the answers/suggestions/whatever. I usually do this in a different colour. Sometimes you need to discuss one last bit maybe, but at least the call is half the length.

SAVE TIME BY
BATCHING TASKS TOGETHER

How long does it take to stop reading this book, reply to an email, sort the post then read a letter and get back into the flow of the book again? Apart from the added stress of jumping between so many different tasks, it's not just the time it takes. What's often not considered is the amount of time it takes from being in the flow doing one task, stop doing that, start doing something else, then get into the flow of the new task. I call this 'set up time'. The way to avoid this grey area of uselessness is to batch tasks together.

The idea of batching tasks together is nothing new, but here's the gist of it. Think about all the things you do multiple times a day/week/month, group them all together and do them in one go. Instead of letting your phone and inbox run your day, how about you run it instead? Try doing all phone calls at say 3pm and emails at set points throughout the day. Do things on your time, not everyone else's. I'll give you some examples of things I batch:

- Reading/responding to email (three times a day)
- Checking post (once every 3 weeks)
- Cooking (once every 2 weeks - yes really!)
- Phone calls (once a day)
- Invoicing (once a week if at all)
- Cleaning (once a week I have a real clean up)
- Writing blog posts (once every 4 months)
- Running errands (every 3 days)
- Shooting videos (whenever I'm on holiday)

Do you get the idea? What I want you to do on the next page is have a think about all the different things you do in a day, week and month. Every single task. Then as I've done, put in brackets how often you could do them. You can ignore the boxes for now, we'll use those later. You'll never shift your day to work like this immediately, but pick the easiest to implement from your list and action it starting today.

BATCHING TASKS TOGETHER

BATCHING TASKS TOGETHER

If you can do this, you'll enjoy a feeling of getting into the zone far more often which makes your work infinitely better and far more enjoyable. As I've said, it's very often the number of things you do in a day that make your day seem complicated, rather than the amount of time you spend doing them.

RUNNING YOUR DIARY
FROM YOUR PHONE OR TABLET

We have discovered an incredible way of syncing your computer with your phone so all your phone calls, reminders and appointments are in one single place. We recommend using Google Calendar. A lot of people use Outlook but frankly, it's an email programme not a reminder system. Google Calendar will sync with a number of different phones. I'm not going to provide instructions to set it up beyond pointing you to some links because by the time this book is published, the software on the phones will have changed and it'll be out of date.

Step 1: Create a Google account

http://accounts.google.com - either log in or create an account

Step 2: Go to Google Calendar

http://calendar.google.com - Then go to settings and set up your mobile phone

Step 3: Sync with your mobile

http://www.google.com/mobile/sync/ - Once you've done this, you're done.

Step 4: Test it

Just add a reminder to Google Calendar at some point in the future, then wait about 15 seconds and check on your phone and the reminder will be there. No wires. No hassle. No post-it notes.

ELIMINATING YOUR MOST TIME CONSUMING TASKS

As a small business owner myself, I understand where most of you are coming from when you say you are busy. You wake up, and the phone rings, you drag yourself around the house to get ready and frantically make it to your first meeting. You finish that, promising someone a proposal, then you get to the office and the phone rings again, you bumble through your day, just about to go home and you realise you forgot to send that guy from this morning his proposal. It's going to take you an hour. Wife has dinner on the table. Kid needs help with homework. What's more important, work or family? What a nightmare!

Let me fix this for you. It's really not hard to do but I need your commitment!

I know this is a bit of a one-way conversation at this point but have you been doing the exercises? If not, sort it out! You need to do this one if you do nothing else. The good news is you've done the hard bit.

In the last exercise, I had you write down all the tasks you do in the average day, week and month. Now what we need to do is work out which ones you do the most. There's a box on the right for a grade so go down each one, using the grading system below and mark it next to each one:

A = Something you do more than once a day
B = Something you do several times a week
C = Once a week or less

Do that now and then look at your A list. If my experience is anything to go by, these tasks are probably taking up over 50% of your time. I want you to ask yourself the question: Is it possible that you could find someone else to do some of those things, even if a little training from you is required? If the answer is yes, put a circle around it. If it's anything in the following list, put a circle round it regardless of what you think:

- Answering the phone
- Sending letters
- Invoicing
- Bookkeeping
- Basic customer service or support

These are all things you could find someone else to do with less than 2 hours of research. I've already explained in the 'Automate My Finances' section that you can get a Virtual Assistant to do your invoicing and bookkeeping. You can get a company to answer the phones which not only makes you seem like a far bigger company, but they protect your time massively so you can get on and do your most profitable task - taking money off people!

The idea of this exercise is to get you to realise that you're probably spending most of your time doing important but menial tasks, not revenue generating tasks.

It's a tough pill to swallow because until now you've been Superman or Superwoman, and taking a back seat so to speak is damaging to your pride - I understand. I was there once.

Then I realised that real business owners don't invoice people, or answer the main company phone, or do front of line customer service. These are things that should be done by a Junior or a Virtual Assistant of some kind. The sooner you take this plunge, the better off you'll be financially and the more free time you'll have. The only way to do it is by outsourcing things you're not an expert at.

OUTSOURCE EVERYTHING
YOU'RE NOT AN EXPERT AT

In this day and age, it's never been easier to outsource tasks. Most people think of the horrible time we all have when calling the bank and an Indian man comes along thinking he can help with his useless pre-written script...

"Thank you for your informations Mr. Adam, my name is Dave, how can I offer you my best service providings?"

"No, your name is definitely not Dave, and I don't want your service providings!"

What most people don't realise is that there are other countries in the world you can outsource things to besides India and they don't have to answer your phones. In fact, I would heavily recommend you didn't outsource anything involving vocal chords to any Indian sounding countries. Ever. I'm not being racist, but our high street Banks have done a terrible job of outsourcing customer service and we have now all had a bad experience with it. A small company following in their footsteps would give off the worst first impression ever.

We primarily use Romania, Poland, and remote parts of America and Canada. None of them touch a phone for us. Having outsourced over 5,000 jobs to date, we have a pretty solid idea of who to use for which jobs, also what kind of thing you can outsource. Anything you can apply logic to and write instructions for will usually be things that can be outsourced successfully. Invoicing is easy for example: "Invoice this customer this amount, on this date, for this service and send a PDF to this email address, and copy me in". You get the idea. I would start with something really simple and try using Freelancer.com or Elance.com. There you'll find cheap per-hour and per-project pricing for simple tasks. If they're good, keep them onboard and involve them more.

Outsourcing doesn't always mean sending it out to remote parts of the planet. Here are some examples of things you should outsource to someone local:

Design and Print:
Don't try to do this yourself, and certainly don't try to design it yourself, unless you are a designer. Leave it to the professionals.

Accounting:
Get a good accountant, do good bookkeeping using Xero and get your accountant to just do your annual accounts. Any good accountant will save you their fees by reducing your tax liability, should you be fortunate enough to be making a profit and be in a position to pay tax.

Videos:
Yes your iPhone shoots in HD but it doesn't make you a professional videographer. Hire a professional.

Photography:
Same thing - Spending a few hours with a professional photographer will get you photos you can use for years to come.

Legal and other Professional Services:
It's just not worth doing this yourself, certainly not for anything complicated.

I'm sure there are tons of examples where you can start outsourcing. It's worth spending the money on these things because it's what these people do day in, day out. Botching it to save yourself a few hundred quid here and there is just not worth the hassle. Hire professionals and enjoy the process of selecting someone. Apart from anything else, you feel like a much bigger business and you look awesome to your customers with the end result!

SUMMARY
OF CHAPTER 9

Any well automated business starts with a well automated business owner. You can't automate everything but you can be more productive, and try to keep that level of efficiency running throughout the business. It makes it more enjoyable to do your work, more enjoyable to buy from you and more enjoyable to work there. It's a hard thing to do, but continuing to improve the business, improving your productivity and improving the systems are all part of having a business that you can be proud of. Lastly, it's your job to do it.

So over the last 9 chapters we've taken a look at your business problems, put some groundwork plans in place to make workflow more efficient and taken a look at some web based software.

We've then looked at a whole host of ways you can automate your Marketing, Sales, Operations, Finance and lastly Yourself. So where do we go from here?

Ultimately you need to make a choice. You can carry on doing what you've been doing, and getting the same results. You could have a fleeting look at some of the apps I've recommended and shelf it because you're busy…

Or you could attack this like it's **life or death** because you know what? It is.

Chapter 10

Evolution

"It's in your moments of decision that your destiny is shaped"

Tony Robbins - Peak Performance Coach

TAKING
ACTION

This book has given you the tools you need to get you from a place of being stressed out your eyeballs, back to things being organised and streamlined. Now you know you don't need to be doing daft admin work, and can focus on what you should be focused on which is driving sales, working on marketing the business and creating strategic alliances with businesses to grow your network.

Once you've implemented the ideas in this book, depending on the growth of your business and the rate at which you'll need these systems to adapt, you may begin to outgrow them. If you reach that point, consider working with a company who can help you identify the deep rooted problems within your organisation, and create you a system which doesn't just organise your business, it automates your business.

I wrote this book to be an educator; something that would take your current approach to organising your company and give it some structure. Then give you some fast action ideas you can implement over a weekend, which would make a radical impact in the way you go about your day to day activities. The question remains, what about once you've done all that and you hit the glass ceiling again?

Businesses are designed to grow and evolve. If they didn't, you'd have a new problem: Being broke! That said, you need to find a system, or set of systems that can grow and evolve at the same rate as your business or you'll find your company being unable to grow.

Most of our clients now use a custom built web based system which manages massive chunks of their businesses on autopilot, leaving them to focus on marketing, promotions, networking and strategic growth - the things a business owner should be doing.

What we do is not a commodity, you won't find us in the Yellow Pages, in any business directories or find 'Business Automation' in any drop down boxes. It's difficult for people to realise a service like this exists. In fact, I've not found any company that does what we do, and I've spent a long, long time searching!

That said, you aren't to blame if you're running around like a chicken with your head cut off, because it's not like your friends are down the pub are saying:

"Oh Matt, what you need is a web based automation system that runs your business on autopilot".

What do you get instead?

"Yeah mate, well that's what happens when you run a business, you have to work long hours".

Hmmm, maybe it's time to stop taking advice from your drinking buddies? It's not your fault you're in the position you're in now, but it is your fault if you know about a way to fix it and you ignore it.

WHAT HAPPENS IF YOU DO ABSOLUTELY NOTHING?

Unfortunately I've seen people split up with girlfriends, families fall apart, people move away, people hit bankruptcy, work themselves almost into a grave and for the sake of what? Pride? Not wanting to delegate through fear of someone else not doing it as well? It's time to think about what your business will look like in 5 years if you do nothing and what it ***could*** look like in 5 years if you have a steady growth plan, not only in revenue but if your systems keep up with sales growth too.

Please do not become another statistic of failed businesses. If you've read this far, it's pretty likely that you've at some point searched for help somewhere along the way. You might not remember, but I know my marketing and it's unlikely you would have found this book if you hadn't been looking for help one way or another. It's your duty to make your business all it can be. Get the help of professionals in every area you can.

In our business, when we find someone struggling who's open to our ideas and help, we sit down with them and go through our Discovery Process. It's at this point we ask a ton of questions and try to identify weak spots with their processes. Using select customised ideas from this book and any new ideas we've come up with since publishing, we make a series of recommendations for free, and simply offer a price for implementation, but it's all free advice. The reason we do this is two-fold:

Firstly, I think if we demonstrate that we have solid ideas and they work, people will want us working on their business systems with them.

Thankfully the people we've worked with enjoy their shorter work weeks, remote working environments and automated businesses. In addition, they keep coming back to us for upgrades and further requests to help with processes they want to streamline, now they've experienced how much time it can save. We must be doing something right.

The second reason is more personal. I've seen a few personal friends and family members struggle with the things I've mentioned in this book, and it's not ended well for them. If I can offer some people just a few ideas for free and it saves them having horrible lives, then I feel I've done my bit. I don't run a charity, but I like to help people and thankfully, enough people buy from us for it to be financially viable for us to do this.

I'm always open to talking to people about these ideas so if you want to talk, I'm not hard to find, my contact details are below. I'd love to meet you at some point and see if any of our ideas can help you and maybe, just maybe, one day we can work together. Either way, I want to really thank you for taking the time to read this book; and I hope more than anything that a few of the ideas make a positive difference in your life. Like anyone putting work out there into the world, I'd love to hear what you think so please send me an email, it would be great to hear from you.

A SMALL CHANGE TODAY
CAN MAKE A HUGE DIFFERENCE

Let me leave you with this thought: a very small change today can make an enormous difference in 6 months, 12 months, 5 years, even 10 years. But it all starts with you **deciding** to make that small change today. If you don't, you'll always wonder what could have been. You must have heard the saying "It's better to regret something you've done than something you haven't". This really applies here. Don't add to the regret or mystery in your life's history by procrastinating. You're in business to be the best you can be right? If not, why are you reading this book? Turn back to Chapter 1, pick up a pen and fill in the spaces I've left for you to plan your amazing future!

Remember to send me an email if this book has helped you in any way. I promise to reply personally.

Thank you again and I wish you all the best.

To a simpler life,

Adam Hempenstall
Founder of The Business Automation Company

Email: adam@businessautomation.co.uk
Office: 0208 123 8413
Mobile: 07793 823301